Cornwall's HAUNTED HOUSES

Margaret Caine & Alan Gorton

For further information of all the titles in this series please visit:-
www.tormark.co.uk

Designed by Alix Wood, www.alixwood.co.uk

Published by Tor Mark, United Downs Ind Est, Redruth,
Cornwall TR16 5HY

First published 2012

ISBN 978 085025 428 0

Printed by R Booth Ltd, The Praze, Penryn, Cornwall TR10 8AA

S ome old Cornish houses seem designed to nurture earth-bound spirits. Here is one.

To get to Penfound Manor you have to go through a bewildering maze of banks and hedges ten feet high, more like passages, and the further you go the less you can see. This is not by accident. You are in old smuggling country and these hedges were carefully built and trained to shield the sight of covered wagons and their illicit cargo from the exciseman's gaze. Only seagulls overhead and salt in the air tells you are near the Atlantic. But when you do get there, and look through the wrought-iron tracery gate, seeming to grow out of the flags themselves, is one of the loveliest old houses you have ever seen, low and rambling, diamond-paned glass winking between the fronds of red creeper, the roof uneven with age, moss growing between tiny slates. It is secretive, like something out of a Hansel and Gretel story.

But don't be deceived. Out of this apparent tranquillity the date April 26 has a frightening significance. That is when the restless ghosts it hosts swirl around to re-enact a tragic story.

The very first house here, just one huge single barn-like room, belonged to Queen Edith, wife of Edward the Confessor. It was sufficiently important to be recorded in the Domesday Book, when it was owned by William the Conqueror's half-brother, Robert, Count of Mortain, and soon afterwards the family who took their name from it – it means 'head of a stream' – moved in and stayed here for the next six hundred years. They were a stubborn, quarrelsome lot, but also thrifty, shrewd and hard-working, with pride in their home and their ancestry, good friends but dangerous enemies, arrogant and high-handed but always straightforward.

One went on a Crusade and brought back a powerful charm – a bottle of Holy Water from the River Jordan, no less – which was put up the massive chimney for safe-keeping. No-one ever has dared to see if there is any water left since a curse says whoever removes it will have the chimney stack fall on his head – so every owner since has left well alone. Above all, the Penfounds were loyal. Down the centuries they remained Royalists to the last man and woman. And because of this they were ruined.

During the seventeenth century, Arthur Penfound was an active smuggler, secretly running valuable contraband from Millook Bay up the old west road to his manor, and on one occasion he actually killed an exciseman when he was surprised by a small party of them out to catch him red-handed. Indeed, it may have been Arthur who ordered the hedges and banks around his home to be raised so high. Though benefiting enormously from this illegal 'free trading', he saw no discrepancy in taking the King's side when Civil War broke out, loudly and vehemently defending his monarch and accusing the Parliamentarians of treachery, and even more so when he became head of the family after his own father had been killed at Stratton, nearby, on 5 May 1643 fighting the Roundheads alongside his neighbour Sir Bevil Grenville of the great Stowe Barton estate.

There the Poundstock church registers stop. Nothing unusual about that: many Royalists destroyed parish records to prevent them getting into the hands of their hated enemy and used against them. Presumably this happened here too, as they start again eleven years later at the end of the Commonwealth. That's a pity, as they would have recorded the birth and death of Kate Penfound. But where the records fail us, legend doesn't.

Arthur lived at the manor with his daughter, Kate. Like all the Penfounds, she was high-spirited, romantic, strong-willed, and we can imagine her with a dainty lace collar round her shoulders, running in and out between the shadows of the cool buildings and the sunlight of the garden, or leading her father's horses along the cobbled path that runs straight through the house to the well at the back. More clearly, we can imagine her in her neat, whitewashed bedroom looking out over the lovely courtyard.

And now, for the first time Kate fell in love, deeply, madly in love with John Trebarfoote, the son of their neighbours of nearby Trebarfoote Manor, only three miles away hidden in a steeply wooded valley nearer to the treacherous coastline at Dizzard Point. Though he reciprocated her affections there was a major obstacle – he and his family had declared their support for Parliament. In more normal times Arthur would have been well pleased to match his daughter with a Trebarfoote: after all, one of Kate's great aunts had married a John Trebarfoote in 1598 and that had worked out well. But the war turned neighbour against neighbour. In Penfound eyes the Trebarfootes were loathsome traitors. No matter how much they tried, neither Kate nor John could convince their respective families that their love was more important than political loyalties. Their only recourse was to elope.

One April evening, the 26th to be precise, young Kate gathered up her skirts and, defying her father, climbed through her bedroom window into the arms of her lover waiting in that courtyard below. Tragically, before the young couple were able to slip away, their movements disturbed members of the household. Arthur's notorious Penfound temper flared.

Here the story divides. Some say that Penfound in his blind anger shot them both as they stood locked in each other's arms in the porch. Some say that Arthur Penfound and young John Trebarfoote drew swords and Kate was killed trying to come between them, after which they fought on until both were wounded and died. Then again, still others say that in attempting to come between John and her father Kate was shot and the men fought on until only John was killed. Since records show that Arthur Penfound died quietly at Winkleigh in Devon in 1656, the first and last are the more probable. In the local church at Poundstock is a slate monument to John Trebarfoote, inscribed:

> *That of Trebarfoote may be truly said*
> *The love of mankind here lies buried.*

That doesn't help us either. But each April 26, the anniversary of this tragedy, the ghostly trio re-appear. Kate's ghost comes first, then joins her lover in the courtyard. Occasionally her ashen face can be seen peering from her bedroom window, waiting for John, just as she must have done three hundred and sixty years ago, little thinking that within an hour or so they would both be dead.

Her father appears in various parts of the house and some former residents have been disturbed by the sounds of voices and bangs and crashings coming from the courtyard, which must be much as it was when two young people who passionately loved each other died there.

Poundstock Church

They are, though, not the only Penfounds who haunt the place. Almost three hundred years earlier, on 27 December, 1357, an appalling murder took place in Poundstock's parish church. The clerk, or priest as we would now call him, who was a Penfound, was viciously attacked while conducting a service. What appears to have happened is that some time before, another powerful local family, the Bedruggans, threw out the existing priest and installed their own. The two families, Penfound and Bedruggan, were at loggerheads. The former appealed to the Pope and he ordered the rightful cleric to be re-instated. The Bedruggans were furious. The matter came to a brutal, bloody head. Bishop Grandisson of Exeter, in his register for that year gave an account of what happened:

Certain satellites of Satan, names unknown, on the Feast of St John the Apostle – which makes the crime worse – broke into the Parish Church of Poundstock within our Diocese with a host of armed men during Mass, and before Mass was scarcely completed they furiously entered the Chancel and with swords and staves cut down William Penvou, Clerk. Vestments and other Church ornaments were desecrated with human blood in contempt of the Creator, in contempt of the Church, to the subversion of ecclesiastical liberty and the disturbance of the peace of the realm. Where will we be safe from crime if the Holy Church, our Mother, the House of God and the Gateway to Heaven, is thus deprived of its sanctity?

We don't know what finally aroused the furious wrath of these 'satellites of Satan' – though we can't help wondering – nor even how many parishioners were involved. What we do know is that at this time the district was being regularly plundered by gangs led by powerful landowners. William Penfound seems to have fallen out with the most successful of them.

Two alleged ringleaders, John Bevill and Simon de St Gennys, were arrested and put on trial. Whatever excuse they gave for bursting into the church and slaughtering the priest before his own altar, again we don't know, but it must have carried weight as they were both pardoned. But not surprisingly after such a dreadful deed, the unavenged ghost of poor 'William Penvou, Clerk,' has wandered ever since among the graves and around the church he loved, sometimes kneeling before the altar, sometimes walking along the path to where he met his death – the church where Kate and John worshipped, walked together in the churchyard, and fell in love.

Dockacre House - Launceston

Launceston was a particular favourite of Poet Laureate Sir John Betjeman, who thought it *the most interesting inland town in Cornwall*, mainly because of its Georgian houses and the amazing parish church. And it's to one of those Georgian houses and the parish church that we go. Dockacre House, in Dockacre Hill, appears an incongruous setting for a tale of horror, but it certainly harbours one. It concerns Elizabeth Herle who died on Christmas Day, 1714.

Originally dating from Elizabethan times, the house was extensively 'renovated' during the reign of Queen Anne, and modified further in early Georgian times. It is an unusual property, long and narrow, built into the side of a hill, and at one time was the home of Revd Sabine

Baring-Gould, who in his novel *John Herring* wrote about a ghost appearing at the front door.

A century and a half before, a noted barrister of his day, Nicholas Herle, lived here with his wife Elizabeth, daughter of the rector of Northcote. Herle was a man of considerable means and political influence, was twice Mayor of London in 1716 and 1721, Mayor of Launceston and High Sheriff of Cornwall. Pastel portraits of the couple, Nicholas and Elizabeth, have hung in the dining room since their time and have always been sold as fixtures with the house. But in the parish church of St Mary Magdalene a secret memorial to Elizabeth was found behind an organ loft which hints at the mysterious circumstances in which she died:

Depart ye life 25 Dec 1714 by starvation or other unlawful means.

Before then, possibly because of their relationship, poor Elizabeth had become mentally deranged. Her husband had her locked away in a small upstairs room where, following one of the prescribed cures at that time, he set about systematically starving her of food. Unfortunately he seems to have overdone it. She was kept confined too long on gradually reducing rations until when almost dead she escaped. As she was making a frantic, frenzied dash for freedom down the stairs, her husband – accidentally or intentionally – shot her.

For more than two hundred years the large, dark stain of Elizabeth's blood marked the second tread up the fine staircase from the hall, and defied all efforts to remove it. Only when new treads were put in, to replace those wearing and becoming dangerous, was the evidence of the 'everlasting bloodstain' removed.

One might have expected Elizabeth to haunt Dockacre House, but oddly it is the ghost of the murderer and not the victim who does so. Even stranger, because Nicholas died on 4 August 1728, not here but at Hampstead, London, two hundred miles away. Nonetheless his ghost has been seen, usually in the beautifully panelled main hall. He has also been heard playing a flute. But be warned because hearing his tune – always the same – is said to predict a death in the family who own the property at that time.

There is another frightening feature of this flute. No ordinary mortal can play it as one end has long been blocked up and it has been made into a walking stick. In fact walking sticks have played a significant role at Dockacre House. A tradition has been maintained over many generations that a departing owner always hands a walking stick to his successor. This is added to the accumulating collection, which now includes a sword stick, a stick with a detachable knob for secreting poison – and the flute stick.

Moreover, they are all kept in a sack in an attic and that in itself has been subject to supernatural activity, for if they are not put away in a particular sequence they will hurriedly rattle about and sort themselves into the 'correct' order, a job always accompanied by loud tapping. Other things happen too: pictures fall from walls without any apparent reason, strange crashes, bangs and thuds occur at night, unexplained footsteps on deserted stairways and in empty rooms, and opening and closing of doors untouched by human hand and with no wind or draught. Dockacre House is indeed seriously haunted.

C ornwall has had more than its share of eccentric clergymen – and here is one of the oddest. In 1931, Frederick William Densham brought his cut-glass accent and lofty Oxford manner to this loneliest of villages. He stayed for twenty-two years.

It was a numerically small parish with only about 2,700 souls in total, but though at first the parishioners found him a little on the strange side, they accepted him. That quickly changed. They realised that this unbending, untidy bachelor could relate to them only according to the letter, as he interpreted it, of Church custom and practice. Soon after his arrival he alienated the Parish Council when he closed the Sunday School. Matters were made worse when he then bought a litter of German Shepherd pups, ostensibly to guard the rectory – but from what was never clear.

The dogs of course grew in size and wandered freely around the village until one of them, named Gandhi after Densham's pacifist hero, but not a vegetarian like its name-sake, teamed up with other dogs to ravage the neighbourhood and killed a sheep – an unforgivable offence in a farming community. Rather than get rid of the dogs, Densham fitted a 600-yard-long barbed-wire fence right round his house, attached to posts eight feet high: to Densham it was the obvious thing to do to prevent it happening again, but it hardly created a welcoming impression.

He painted the rectory walls red, yellow and blue, which to his own way of thinking would uplift the spirits of his congregation, so he painted the interior of the church in the same garish colours. The congregation saw it differently. Next he refused to hold services at times convenient to his parishioners until, only two years after he had arrived, some of them sought to have him sacked. The Bishop of Truro, Dr Walter Frere, presided over an enquiry into the rector's conduct but after arguing that he had done nothing wrong in ecclesiastical law to merit his removal, he was exonerated – despite the secretary of the Church Council accusing Densham of threatening to kill him when he tried to stop him 'improving' the church. The Church Council resigned as a body and resolutely shunned the place. Others followed. Before long no one attended his church, and entries in his Service Book began to read: *No fog, no wind, no rain, no congregation* or *Severe gale with hail. Very cold. No congregation.*

At this impasse, Densham's odd logic came into play yet again – he needed a congregation so what better than to provide his own! In a simple but ingenious measure, he cut figures out of wood and cardboard and propped them up in the church pews, where he preached passionate sermons to his ever-attentive 'flock'. By now he was completely ostracised by the villagers. If anyone did go to the fence to peer into the tangled weeds of the rectory garden they glimpsed a dark-coated figure pacing endlessly up and down the drive, hands clasped behind his back, head bowed in deep thought, wearing a strange old-fashioned shovel hat.

Throughout, he neglected the rectory. Always cold – he tore up the floorboards to make fires and there was not a stick of furniture, as he had burned that, too – it became leaky and dilapidated. Over the years, Densham became practically a hermit. His only visitors were the occasional postman and a fortnightly call from a Bodmin grocer who left oats, butter and margarine in a box at the entrance to the rectory grounds. He lived entirely on porridge (villagers believed he added nettles to it) – never fish or flesh. When on Christmas Day, 1952, he preached a sermon based on 'God is Love', not a single living soul heard it. No one showed the slightest compassion or extended a hand of friendship.

Ironically, Densham's eccentricity and his ostracisation within his own parish became newsworthy. In the New Year of 1953 two reporters and a photographer from the *Western Morning News* and the American weekly *Life* attended his service. They were the only ones. A few days later, some villagers noticed that the rectory chimney was not smoking as usual, and no-one had seen him heading for his daily services in the empty, decaying church or pacing the drive beyond the high fence. They tried to attract his attention by banging on the gate and calling out, but received no response.

The police were sent for. They found his body in a crumpled heap at the foot of the stairs, where he had fallen and died. Some say he had an expression of dreadful horror on his dead face, but this may have been just to add a Gothic touch. Knowing his end was near – he was now 83 years old – he had put a pile of apples on a table ready to distribute them to the parish sick. In this final act of charity he had slipped. He had been dead at least two days. Even his last wishes were ignored. Instead of his ashes being scattered as he asked in the private Garden of Remembrance he had created in the rectory grounds, they were placed in a public garden in Plymouth. One wish was readily granted though: no memorial marks his resting place.

But the mark Revd Frederick William Densham left was deep and enduring. In fact he is still with us. On moonlit nights, as owls hoot in nearby trees, a sad, dark figure walks where he walked so often in life towards the empty church, perhaps to see if he has a congregation at last. Sometimes, in his torn cassock and dusty hat, he sits where he used to sit and preaches where he used to preach. Sometimes he walks dolefully up the drive and rambles around the rectory (now *The Rookery*, converted into flats). Sometimes he is in the garden in his long black coat and with the walking stick he was so reluctant to be seen using.

Actually, his is not the first ghost here. Long before Revd Densham, Ralph de Tremur lived in a building on the same site and his ghost can be seen from time to time. He is said to have celebrated Black Masses in the church and burned the Host publicly. After resigning the living in 1334, Ralph briefly returned to rob the new rector and burn down his rectory. No wonder his heretical opinions and intractable behaviour were castigated by Bishop Grandisson of Exeter:

O detestable tongue, more poisonous than that of a mad dog
which ought to be cut out by the surgeons of Church and Crown
and be chopped up and thrown to the pigs!

With such tenacious ghosts and darkest of memories, small wonder Warleggan is haunted.

Jamaica Inn - Bolventor

I*nto Bodmin and out of this world* was an old saying reflecting perfectly the somewhat brooding atmosphere of the former county capital. Don't linger in the town too long, though, Bodmin Moor is waiting for you. Celtic crosses lean wearily into the relentless, howling wind; stone circles huddle together for comfort; shells of abandoned mine engine houses cast forlorn silhouettes against the sky. It's a place where your imagination can run away with you. No wonder, 150 years ago all but the most stout-hearted of travellers tended to avoid it. It was not just the fear of thieves or highwaymen – there was something hostile about it, something of deferred foreboding. Even now it can be truly lonely and those who work and farm here can be cut off for days by incessant lashing rain or the eerie, woolly silence of its capricious, sudden mists and gulping mires.

Isolated on the old coach road between Launceston and Bodmin, and before that a carriers' track, is *Jamaica Inn* at Bolventor, infamously immortalised by Daphne du Maurier in her eponymous novel of murder, violence, passion, loss and a terrifying landlord: the gothic gloom and suspense she created captures its essence perfectly. More recently it was claimed in the April, 2004, TV programme *Most Haunted* as 'the spookiest place' the presenters had ever visited, with no less than 15 ghosts becoming apparent during the investigation.

The inn was built in 1547 as a farm, then in 1750 became a coaching inn, where travellers whose weary lot was to traverse the turnpike over the wild and treacherous tableland of course pasture and waste sedges could get shelter and sustenance, and horses could be changed after their long slog over the rough road. In 1778 it was extended to include a coach house, stables and a tack room creating the L-shaped main part of the building we see today, before becoming a Temperance House and more recently reverting to a fully-licensed inn. Its unlikely name came from the local landowning Trelawney family, two of whose members served as Governors of Jamaica in the eighteenth century, though why they retired here is anybody's guess – or did it get it from the considerable trade it did in contraband rum?

Smugglers stopped here on their journeys across the moor or to hide the goods they had secreted ashore. One estimate says that half the brandy and a quarter of the tea smuggled into the UK was landed on the coasts west of here, so the isolation of *Jamaica Inn* made it an ideal staging post for some of it. Since those days it has changed little. The wind-lashed courtyard in front is still cobbled, over which stagecoaches used to rattle. Mysterious hoof-beats of a coach and horses pulling up sometimes clatter on them today, and on occasion sounds have been heard of heavy objects being unloaded, with creaking from the springs of a cart or carriage, though witnesses woken by these noises and whinnying of horses see nothing, while on foggy nights the figure of a man on horseback waits outside for some-one unknown.

The sign swings and creeks in the breeze, the great wooden door beneath the porch leads to an interior of sloping floors and fireplaces with roughly-cut granite lintels. In one corner a doorway leads into 'Mary's Bar', named after Mary Yellan, the heroine of du Maurier's story. It was at this bar that a stranger stood drinking a pot of ale. He was never to finish it. This old seaman had arrived and ordered a meal. Waiting for it to be prepared, he took his half-full tankard outside into the pale sunlight and sat on the stone boundary wall surrounding the courtyard. He must have just completed a voyage for he had a large, bulging sack with him – and this caught the eye of some of the thieves who infested the moor, where they were far from justice.

When his meal was ready, the stranger went inside with his sack but one of the thieves lured him outside again. Was it talk of a pretty girl or someone anxious to see his goods which made him follow? We shall never know what trick was used but he put down his tankard and disappeared into the night. There the gang fell on him. Next morning his lifeless corpse was found, but his identity has never been discovered. Since his ghost was first reported in 1911, many people have seen a strange man sitting, silent and motionless, on the wall.

He doesn't respond to greetings, appears oblivious to those who pass him by, and after a few moments of gazing nonchalantly into space slowly dissolves into nothingness, but his description is so similar to that of the stranger who was murdered for his sack of goods that it must be him. Then at certain times of the year ghostly footsteps echo on the stone floors along the passage near 'Mary's Bar'. Are they of the dead man periodically returning to finish his last drink? Ghosts of smugglers have certainly been heard, sometimes shouting, sometimes talking in strong Cornish dialect.

Then there is a green-cloaked man who walks from the restaurant through a heavy panelled door to the Reception area. On other occasions footsteps have been heard late at night walking along an upstairs corridor and into the last bedroom door on the right. This is the same bedroom where the spectre of a man can be seen. He is always wearing a tricorn hat and a long, old-fashioned, tight-waisted overcoat and saunters slowly past the end of the bed before disappearing through a large wardrobe, leaving the room icy cold – additional to *Jamaica Inn*'s normal brooding atmosphere.

Whether the two ghosts are connected in some way, as well as that cloaked one which has been seen on numerous occasions in the kitchen of the stable block, we don't know but they are all part of the repertoire. One may even be a highwayman, Jack Trevellis, who was supposedly around here in 1791 and whose portrait hangs on the wall of the inn, though we have been unable to find any historical records to verify this. However, one of the most recent and frequent apparitions is that of an anguished young mother and her baby who haunt room 5, and have been reported many times to walk through the wall where the mirror is now.

Science cannot explain such experiences, but they leave us much to ponder over. We just have to accept there is no convincing explanation.

O f Cornwall's many great houses, Lanhydrock must rank as one of the foremost. It is a visual treasure, set in rolling, wooded countryside alongside the River Fowey. For centuries until it was surrendered to Henry VIII in 1539, the estate had been one of the many possessions of the huge Augustinian Priory of St Petroc in Bodmin, was acquired by the Glynn family from whom it passed by marriage to the Lyttleton and Trenance families, before being bought by the family who were to live here over the next 300 years. They hailed from Truro and were just plain Roberts then, but from a fairly humble background trading first in wood and furze to fuel the county's tin furnaces, then in wool and tin and money lending, by the time Richard Roberts sealed the family's social position by buying the Lanhydrock estate in 1620 he had been High Sheriff in 1614 and created a knight two years later, became a baronet five years after that and was finally ennobled as Baron Robartes of Truro (note the subtle but deliberate change of name) in 1625.

It was he who in 1630 began to replace the old farm with a mansion reflecting his standing, a house of wealth and power, completing it in 1642. His son John, the second Lord Robartes, despite his earlier support for Parliament in the Civil War, was given an Earldom (of Radnor) by King Charles II. Another outstanding member was Thomas James Robartes who inherited the property from his mother and lived here during most of the nineteenth century. He was the owner of several tin and copper mines in west Cornwall but still found time to make further improvements to his estate. It was a cruel irony then when on 4 April 1881 a disastrous fire gutted almost the whole house.

The *West Briton* reported: *As night came on the scene was one of weird grandeur. Some of the timbers were still occasionally bursting into flame in the boisterous wind.* Few thought the spectacle so picturesque. It had begun in the kitchen roof, but the conflagration took hold so rapidly that Lady Robartes, then aged 68, had to be rescued by climbing through an upstairs window and scrambling down a ladder to avoid being incinerated. She never got over the shock or the effects of smoke and died only a few days later. Her husband did not long survive her. The loss of his wife and home was too great, and within a year, overwhelmed by grief, he followed her to the grave. Immediately, their son, Thomas, had the house rebuilt, keeping to the outer form of the original (minus the east wing which had been removed a hundred years earlier) but furnishing it in Jacobean style and incorporating the latest advances in late-Victorian technology.

To this day the house exudes an air of serenity. That belies its being haunted by an impressive array of ghosts. One is of a little, gentle old 'Grey Lady' in a long dress who wafts through the rooms, particularly the seventeenth-century Long Gallery, the great room running the length of the house, interestingly a remnant of the original house pre-dating the dreadful fire. She is so solid she is often taken to be a real person until she slowly fades away.

In this Gallery, at the far end on the right-hand side, is a small hinged window of stained glass dated 1675. John, 2nd Earl of Radnor, married Lady Lucy Rich, daughter of the second Earl of Warwick, and later Isabella (Letitia), daughter of Sir John Smith. Despite bearing him fourteen children, John guarded his young wife jealously – with good cause. The earl was frequently away and his wife was equally frequently visited by the then Duke of York, so the earl had her fitted with a chastity belt. At all events, the beautifully decorated little glass appears to depict the Devil attempting to remove the belt while the Duke (or is it her husband?) looks on. Little is known about it other than it was found near the church, though the ghostly 'Grey Lady' does seem to be walking towards it. Strictly speaking, no-one knows her identity but many think she is Isabella.

Yet other female Robartes put in appearances. One, more a presence than an apparition, has been experienced in Her Ladyship's Room, and is thought to be the Lady Robartes who was rescued at the time the house was virtually gutted by the violent fire. Another has a rather convoluted story. Apparently, a former Lord Robartes was an inveterate gambler and one night, half in jest, offered his daughter in marriage as his stake in a card game. Rather than marry the man who 'won' her, the daughter committed suicide by jumping from the tower, and she now haunts the little room at the top of the house which had been her bedroom.

There are, though, snags to this explanation: that particular room was part of the Victorian servants' quarters and never a high-status bedroom; none of the Robartes family gambled a daughter, and only one, a boy, Alexander Agar-Robartes, is known to have committed suicide, and that was between the wars. But perhaps the story has humbler origins, in the suicide of the 22-year-old Annabelle O'Connor, an Irish maid who had become pregnant by a fellow employee who was already married. Whichever it is, one of them certainly haunts the tower room.

As if these were not enough, there is the ghost of a sixteenth-century Catholic priest wracked with guilt over his affair with a female domestic and the baby son subsequently born to her; that of a man hanged outside the Gatehouse by the Royalist army in the Civil War after being accused of robbing the house, dragged swiftly outside and his body left on display; that of a ten-year-old girl called Emily who died of a heart problem in the 1760s; that of a teenage boy who had been trampled to death by a horse in 1795; that of a maidservant who died after falling downstairs in the 1820s; that of a toddler who perished from scarlet fever at about the same time; that of a former head butler called Albert Leah who died of natural causes around 1890; that of a small boy called Robert who liked to play hide-and-seek in the Luggage Room; that of a cheerful tailor who also cleaned the household's shoes; and that of a dapper gent wearing Victorian clothes complete with top hat and blue waistcoat who may be linked to the fire or simply a former resident of the house, still wandering his former home. There are still more. In particular, lights have been seen moving around a particular book – the *Brevium Romanum*, a book of Latin prayers and readings published in 1568 – in the Long Gallery.

So as you walk around, keep your eyes peeled, your ears alert, and your mind open! The Robartes family line ran out in 1969, by which time the house and grounds had been in the care of the National Trust for sixteen years – but that hasn't prevented them making their presences felt!

St Petroc's - Padstow

U ntil quite recently, the room at the top of the rickety stairs of the Padstow Institute in Broad Street housed the local museum. One of its exhibits was an old one pound note declaring *LODENEK BANK – Thomas Rawlings & Son, 1801*, promising to pay the bearer in cash if it was presented at Coutts & Co., London. Therein lies a tale – and a haunting.

The Rawlings family almost exemplified the adage of rags to riches and back again in three generations. Originally they lived in St Columb as small-scale but successful agricultural merchants, until in 1770 William Rawlings moved his family to Padstow, where one of his sons, the evangelical William, was vicar. This was a time when the port was becoming increasingly busy, handling coastal and foreign cargoes, and had a thriving ship-building business with all the ancillary trades. Some time during the 1790s William's other son, Thomas, then just over 30 years of age, branched out into an import-export business and was soon bringing tallow, hemp and canvas from St Petersburg, pit props from Norway and Sweden, coal from South Wales and lime from Ireland; in return he exported slate from nearby quarries, tin and copper ores and other minerals from local mines, fish caught in surrounding waters, and agricultural produce brought by inland farmers. It seemed that whatever they became involved in, the Rawlings family were successful. Catches of fish were sold in bulk and Thomas's fish brokering business was so successful that the *Royal Cornwall Gazette* of January 1802 carried an advert:

> For Sale at the Golden Lion 90 hogsheads of pilchards,
> further details from Mr T Rawlings.

He worked hard, prospered, added a ships' chandlery to his business, and in almost no time at all had a hand in most aspects of the port's life. As a consequence, Thomas was appointed Vice-Consul for Sweden, Norway and the Netherlands to look after the interests of sailors and cargoes from those countries, and within ten years of his arrival was establishing his own private bank here in the town, the Lodenek Bank. Before long he owned two inns, three warehouses, several farms, a shipwrights' yard and a number of properties including St Petroc's, halfway up the hill from the harbour. This last he didn't buy as a commercial proposition to let like the others, but to house his growing family which by 1806 had reached a total of fifteen children (with three others buried by their uncle, the vicar, in the churchyard before their second birthdays).

Having involved his son, another William, in his business, Thomas Rawlings & Son flourished. The family were upwardly mobile. The outlook was rosy. First, Thomas became a Justice of the Peace, then a High Sheriff of Cornwall and latterly Deputy Lord Lieutenant. It was now that he decided to build a Regency-style mansion to rival Prideaux Place itself, on land he owned at Sandy's Hill overlooking the town. While William took over their old home at St Petroc's in early 1818, the others moved into their new house. They were there less than three years. And their outlook was anything but rosy.

On 22 July 1820, aged 63, Thomas died. His family's grief was compounded when William examined his father's accounts and discovered huge debts, well over £100,000, brought about by overspending on public duties but also by a decline in trade as St Ives, Hayle, Falmouth and Fowey – all nearer to the main mining districts – became competitors, while his farms had become liabilities. William, now 32 years old, had to find the money, and find it quickly. He had little room for manoeuvre.

Over the next two years the new grand mansion was sold, just breaking even, while other properties including St Petroc's, the farms lock, stock and barrel, the shipwrights' yard with all its timber, equipment and tools, and all except one of the warehouses, went under the auctioneer's hammer. The bank closed. William was left with just what his father had started with. Cap in hand he negotiated a lease with St Petroc's new owners, and here he brought his mother and three unmarried sisters, with a few long-standing servants to look after them in their very reduced circumstances.

Two of William's sisters, Emma aged 19 and Jenny aged 17, readily adjusted, but Annie, aged 22, found the move and her new life difficult. It was worse when the Hussars major to whom she had become engaged broke off the relationship. Annie took to her room and refused to come out for days at a time.

Fortunately for them all, William had a good head for business. Over the years he nursed the family firm back to health, was made a JP and later, like his father, appointed a Deputy Lord Lieutenant of Cornwall. But life was never the same. In 1828 Jenny married a small tenant farmer but Annie refused to attend the ceremony: such a match was below her expectations both for Jenny and most certainly for herself – she would prefer to remain a spinster. After both her mother and one of her brothers, Revd Rawlings, vicar of Lansallos, died in 1835, Annie even stopped going to church. Soon she stopped going out altogether. Her daily routine changed too, sleeping all morning and wandering through the house at night: there was more than one occasion when the servants mistook her for a ghost and screamed in fright. By the age of 40 she was a recluse. Folk forgot her. Gossips said she had gone insane.

In 1840, William Rawlings died. After years of unremitting hard work, all he left was just enough to provide for his own two sons and his unmarried sisters, Annie and Eliza, but they would have to leave St Petroc's. Annie refused. She refused even to discuss it and had to be given an ultimatum: either move to a smaller house, one of their former ostler's cottages, with Eliza or be certified insane and placed in a lunatic asylum.

Notwithstanding the horrors of many Victorian asylums and the social stigma, what is not generally known is that privately-funded people could go into the one at Bodmin to live in reasonable accommodation and receive sympathetic attention from the staff. Her nephew Walter was less sympathetic: after Annie had brooded on her situation for three weeks he demanded she make up her mind, as new tenants were waiting to move into the house and the family must move out. In the early hours of that night, Annie went to the kitchen and hanged herself.

Annie was not buried with the other members of the Rawlings family in their plot with their head-stones along the south wall of Padstow parish church. As a suicide she was buried in unconsecrated ground outside the churchyard walls. Nor was her name recorded on any of the three marble and six brass Rawlings family plaques you can see inside, along with her sisters, Charlotte (aged 28), Fanny (54), Kitty (81), Jenny (89), Eliza (79) and Emma (78) – no Annie.

Over the next hundred and fifty years or so St Petroc's had mixed fortunes. Under a succession of tenants it was allowed to deteriorate until rescued and restored by new owners, after which it became a hotel. It witnessed an equal amount of activity inside. Many of the tenants and guests have actually seen a tall, slim lady with a pale, oval face and large, listless eyes, greying reddish hair loose about her head, wearing a long grey dress and bodice with a fiche collar, her posture upright and her demeanour imperious as she climbs one of the staircases or moves along one of the corridors nearby.

Sometimes she fades away as they approach, but mostly she vanishes through a wall at the end of the passageway where previously there had been a door. She has been seen in a rocking chair in the kitchen but has got up and left, unspeaking, as soon you go in – but again through the wall. It seems that Miss Annie Rawlings was particularly fond of the kitchen. When she was alive, she used to creep down at night to warm herself, sit in the cook's rocking chair and reflect on her past life, once so full of promise, never fulfilled. Now her ghost does the same.

St Petroc's has been considerably altered inside since the days of the Rawlings but the exterior is much the same and you can see why it was such a desirable property for a commercially successful family. Its Georgian pillared doorway and large sash windows mark it out as befitting merchants, ship-builders and well-to-do folk. If you feel sufficiently confident you may wish to take a peek inside – Annie Rawlings will be around somewhere!

Penrose Manor - Sennen

R ationally, we can't explain why half a million people visit the wind-swept Land's End promontory each year. Perhaps it's because the meeting of the Atlantic Ocean and the English Channel produce some of the most hazardous coastal waters in Britain. Perhaps it's the ghosts.

The manor house at Penrose took its name from the family who owned it, and its history is rather complex. Some three or four hundred years ago, one of them, Ralph Penrose, was so grief-stricken when his wife died of an illness that he decided to travel abroad, taking his seven-year-old son, Stephen, and his cousin William, leaving his estate to be managed by his younger brother, John.

One night though their boat ran into a storm and foundered on the rocks just below here, actually within sight of his house. Flares alerted local people to what was happening but, on John's explicit instructions and afraid to disobey, they stood, watched and did nothing to help. Only Stephen survived, washed onto the shore. John knew full well that his time as master of the estate was under threat if this rightful heir lived, so he callously murdered his nephew.

However, William too had managed to get ashore. Thinking he was the only one, and with no wish to settle in the area William went abroad again until one day, quite by chance, he turned up at Penrose. It was here he heard Stephen's voice: *My uncle murdered me … avenge the murder of your cousin's son … dig beneath the dead tree in the orchard, and give me peace*. Helped by a long-standing friend, William unearthed the remains of the murder victim. That night, they carried them to Sennen church and re-buried them in an unmarked plot.

Back at Penrose they found the body of John Penrose hanging from a beam. He had seen that Stephen's makeshift grave had been disturbed and committed suicide in sight of it. This meant that William was now the owner, and for a time he lived at the manor house but was so haunted by what had happened that he gave up all rights to it and went on his wanderings abroad again, where eventually he died.

Stephen no longer haunts the house. His spirit settled after he was buried in Sennen churchyard. But the ghost of his uncle John does, appearing regularly in the room where he hanged himself, presumably searching forever for a way to assuage his guilt, deep, coruscating, soul-destroying guilt. Or is he the reflection of some dark, strange place in our mind that our modern world hasn't touched?

First & Last Inn - Sennen

While you are in this area, we feel sure you will wish to visit the *First and Last Inn*. As soon as you get there you will notice one thing: it's location was ideal for smugglers, who not surprisingly abounded in these parts. And therein lies the cause of a number of ghostly happenings.

In the nineteenth century, the *Sennen Inn* (as it was called then) was owned by a wealthy farmer from Mayon, Dionysius Williams. One of his entrepreneurial activities was to finance smuggling ventures, while the inn's tenant, John George, arranged the landing for his contraband cargoes. However, John George was not the most loyal of employees and tried to blackmail his landlord, refusing to pay his rent and threatening to tell the officers of the law what was going on. Williams was not going to stand for this, so turned him out, whereupon George's wife, Anne, betrayed Williams to the magistrates and he was heavily fined.

Anne George also became King's Evidence against another well-off farmer, Christopher Pollard of Madron, who had a previous conviction for smuggling and in one night had landed 3,000 gallons of brandy before he was caught. But this time her testimony was not accepted. Pollard was acquitted. Soon afterwards a gang of men dragged a screaming Anne George to Sennen Cove where she was tied to a stake on the sands and left to drown in the next incoming tide. From there her body was carted back to the inn and laid out in an upstairs room before being buried in an unmarked grave in the adjacent churchyard.

After such a violent end, it is not surprising that Anne George's ghost haunts the inn, slamming doors or standing beside guests' beds or, wearing long dark clothing, her face time-worn, standing in a corner of the largest bedroom. There have also been inexplicable spillages of spirits and beer in locked rooms, breakages in most of the private areas, and figures on stairways. Anne George's spirit is indeed restless, a notorious lady who paid a heavy price for her betrayal.

Hers is not though the only one here. In a terribly sad incident, a little girl was knocked down and killed by a stagecoach rushing by. Ever since she has haunted room 6, where guests have heard a child's voice asking them to play with her, though no-one seems to have actually seen her.

Pengersick Castle – Praa Sands

Though standing in its own grounds in the broad sweep of countryside just east of Hoe Point, Pengersick Castle may seem now somewhat incongruous amongst the caravan parks of Praa Sands. Despite this, what you see is part of a romantic stronghold with an extraordinary track record of paranormal activity. Indeed, its name has become so synonymous with ghosts that it is officially the most haunted castle in Britain.

In effect, the fifteenth-century fortified tower is all that remains of a once great manor. Though we don't know its exact age, there must have been a building here before the apothecary's garden was developed in the thirteenth century and a manor is mentioned in a document dated 1199 concerning a dispute over land ownership, though sadly the details have been lost. The place took its name from Richard de Pengersick who was murdered in 1221.

His descendant, the first Henry de Pengersick married Engrina Godolphin, whose family owned adjoining estates, and died in 1327, but their son, also Henry, known as 'Henry le Fort', seems to have been an unpleasant character before he died in 1343. He was subject to 'the Greater Excommunication' for attacking and wounding the vicar of Breage and a monk from Hailes Abbey in Gloucestershire when in 1330 they called to collect their tithes. Though Henry never lived in the present building, his ghost and that of the burly monk wearing a black cloak and wide-brimmed hat are among the oldest which haunt it: stones to build the castle were taken from the old manor house, which enabled these ghosts to occupy their new haunting ground. The monk wanders in the castle grounds, often through a wall, and some people have spoken to and heard him confess to a number of misdeeds.

The Pengersick estate received a welcome injection of money when Henry's grand-daughter married John Bevill, but unfortunately fell into decline when their grand-daughter Isabell married Thomas Worth and moved to Devon. However, it passed to their daughter Elizabeth, wife of John Milliton of Meavy, who decided to build a larger and grander castellated and fortified mansion with two courtyards. Many bizarre tales are told of the Millitons, but they went on to play a number of influential roles in the life of the county: their son, John, became Captain of St Michael's Mount in 1522 and both he and his son, William, were Sheriffs of Cornwall.

In fact, the most frequently seen ghost is that of this first John Milliton. Apparently, he had killed a man on the streets of London during a drunken brawl and hid himself away in a private chamber in the tower here for the rest of his life. Locked in a marriage of mutual detestation, he tried to rid himself of a troublesome wife by poisoning her: she, however, suspected his little game and craftily managed to switch the wine goblets, so they succeeded in killing each other simultaneously. Interestingly, there has never been any mention of his wife among the spectral company which haunts his house – just John.

The second John Milliton, now owner of the estate, became involved with his wealthy neighbours William Godolphin and Thomas St Aubyn in the mysterious looting of the King of Portugal's carrack *St Anthony*, which became a political and national *cause célèbre* and even involved King Henry VIII. The ship was wrecked at Gunwalloe in 1526, though its cargo, valued then at £18,000, vanished without trace. Even though the matter became the subject of a Royal Commission, the whereabouts of the untold riches were never discovered. It may have been sealed up in the secret passages of Pengersick, for ever since ghosts of the dead sailors from the wreck have been seen searching for it.

William Milliton and his wife Honor had seven daughters and then a son who they thought would at last be their heir, but he died in tragic circumstances while abroad, so in 1571 the property was divided between the girls. This was an impractical arrangement, the estate declined, the house fell into disuse and all but the fortified tower gradually decayed into a ruin, with the materials used to build neighbouring cottages. Thanks to the labours of more recent owners, this fascinating place has been restored.

The modern wing has been converted into a house while the tower remains in its Tudor state, its thick granite walls holding many secrets. Its interior is unspoilt, with a narrow spiral staircase giving access to a succession of rooms leading eventually to the battlements – where at least one spirit appears, that of a young girl in red who fell off the highest turret while dancing around and now delights in trying to persuade visitors to do the same! Other ghosts seem to be focused on a third floor bedroom and its old four-poster bed. Certainly it is the most haunted room in the house, exuding a weird atmosphere sensed by many people, with 'something' in it. A monk, a knight, two ladies dressed in thirteenth-century fashion and a demon hound have all put in an appearance. Of the female figures, the clearer has been identified as Lady Engrina Pengersick, tall, slim, moving with an aristocratic air and emerging from the bedroom wall, seemingly searching for something. She wears a full-length grey or pale coloured gown fastened by an ornate belt from which hangs a sparking jewel. For the other, the bed itself seems to be the catalyst.

This gaunt phantom bends over to examine those who dare to sleep in it! Some claim a Demon from Hell is present in the room, which was conjured up by John Milliton during one of his occult sessions and has remained to this day, preying on people's fear, living in the fireplace and appearing as an ominous shape of a dog with glowing red eyes. One of the most dramatic sightings by many people, though, is the peculiar misty white vapour, a writhing swirl surging from the four-poster and slowly floating across the room just above floor level before taking on the form of a woman wearing a long sleeved nightgown, patterned below the neckline. She gets off the bed clutching her abdomen as if in pain, then lies down again. At this point another female form wafts through the wall, wearing a textured black, three-quarter length coat over a shiny cream-coloured dress. She glides around as if ministering to the figure prone on the bed.

These are by no means all. The spirit of a woman who was stabbed to death in the fifteenth century appears at the spot of her murder, and a man stabbed and strangled in the sixteenth century appears by the fireplace, while a four-year-old boy often tugs at visiting women's dresses.

You may think that some of these tales of ghostly activity are dubious or even outrageous, but there is much at Pengersick that defies logical, rational explanation from its total of over twenty separate paranormal presences.

In the far west of the county, the Earls of Godolphin built an imposing mansion, leaving us with yet another of those properties particularly attractive to spirits. This one you approach through a narrow avenue of stunted oaks which, on a dull, damp day has the full flavour of a horror film, before it opens out to give a frontal view of the house and its Tuscan columns. This comes as something of an anti-climax: it is open and friendly, an atmosphere which continues inside despite it being haunted.

The most famous ghost here is the 'White Lady' who walks along a path leading from the house to the old chapel. So frequently has she been seen over the years that her route has become known as the 'ghost path'. We can identify exactly who she is and why she is here. She is Margaret, wife of the courtier Sydney Godolphin. You can see her portrait on the library wall inside, bare-armed, fashionably moderately buxom, eyes modestly downcast, but communicating none of the wit and brilliance she displayed in life.

Margaret was born on 2 August 1651, daughter of a Royalist soldier, Colonel Thomas Blagge, a Groom of the Bedchamber to Charles I, who at the time was away fighting at the battle of Worcester. He escaped with the future Charles II, but was captured and imprisoned in the Tower, from where he managed to escape again and make his way to France to rejoin the exiled Court. It was against this background of constant uncertainty and instability that Margaret grew up, partly in France where she had been taken to be looked after by the Countess of Guilford, Groom of the Stole to the exiled Queen Mother, Henrietta Maria.

The Restoration brought only slight improvement. Margaret was nine years old, her father was made Governor of Landguard and Yarmouth, but died shortly afterwards. Though buried in Westminster Abbey, his service to the king had cost him dearly and he died in debt, leaving a widow and four young girls to fend as best they could. Fortunately, by petitioning the new King, Mrs Blagge was granted a pension and her eldest daughter a position at Court. At the age of 14, Margaret became Maid of Honour to the Duchess of York at St James's Palace, and after the latter's death transferred to the service of the Queen, Catherine of Braganza. It was now, at the age of 16, that she first met her future husband.

Sydney Godolphin left Cornwall when he was 17, sent to be a Page of Honour at the Court of Charles II, with a salary of £120 per year. From that he developed a highly successful career, serving in governments under four monarchs from Charles II to Queen Anne, for whom he was Lord High Treasurer and was raised to the peerage as first Earl of Godolphin.

Margaret and Sydney married secretly in May, 1675, at the Temple church in London. Though they proved a devoted, loving couple their ambitions and expectations were different. She wished for a quiet, simple life away from the politicking and intrigue of Court.

He revelled in it just as much as he did the gaming tables and races at Newmarket.

Margaret had already met the diarist and dedicated committee man, John Evelyn, when she was 19 years of age. He was 23 years older. Drawn together initially by their religious leanings, they made an odd pair but their friendship was as genuine as it was intense, with him visiting or their writing to each other as often as three times a week. When she married, Margaret kept the secret even from Evelyn. He was deeply hurt, but it wasn't long before they resumed their flow of correspondence and he produced a 100-page treatise *Oeconomics to a Newly Married Friend*, promising their friendship would *accompany us to the other World, when all Flesh and Blood, yea, and of Marriage it self shall cease.* This tripartite relationship of wife, husband, and Evelyn remains intriguing, though it was clearly platonic and which they regarded as spiritual.

Margaret was now wealthy, highly respected, with a considerable social position, but when she became pregnant her health was affected adversely. In the later stages, she went with her friends John Evelyn and his wife to Lambeth to visit the home of Elias Ashmole and his collection of 'Raritys' (the basis of the Ashmolean Museum at Oxford). After studying his mathematical instruments and books of astrology, Ashmole predicted Margaret would give birth to a boy, 'a brave Child.' Back home, her health deteriorated rapidly. Evelyn was summoned to her bedside as her life ebbed away. On 3 September 1678 she gave birth to a healthy son, Francis, the future second Earl of Godolphin. Six days later on 9 September, despite the attentions of four doctors, *neither the Cupping and the Pidgions* could save her and she died from an infection of the womb. She was twenty-five.

Such an eventuality was not uncommon. Margaret had prepared for it. In a detailed, tender letter she left with her sister-in-law, Mrs Joel Boscawen, to be delivered to her husband if she should 'be to leave this world', she insisted her body be taken to her husband's home for burial, a place she had never visited:

… you will sometime think of me with Kindnesse; but never with too much Griefe: For my Funerale, I desire there may be no Cost bestow'd upon it at All. I would Begg, that my Bodie might lie, where I have had such a mind to Go myself … I believe, if I were Caryed by Sea, the Expense would not be very Greate …

It was not to be. Margaret's embalmed body was brought, not as she had asked, but by the more expensive land route, and funeral costs were 'not much less than £1,000.' In a lead coffin, her last journey in a hearse pulled by six horses, attended by two coaches with thirty of her relatives and servants – but neither her husband nor best friend John Evelyn – took two weeks to cover the distance from London to the parish of Breage, 'the cradle of her husband's race'. One week later, her body was laid beneath the altar in the simple Godolphin Chapel. The epitaph on her tomb was written by Evelyn,

Here lies a Pearle, none Such the Ocean Yields,
  In all the Treasurs of his liquid fields …

From that day her ghost has haunted Godolphin House. It makes an official appearance on the anniversary of her death, September 9, but on other occasions too, usually in the hall where she comes from a tiny closet, long since sealed up, her full white silk dress unmistakeably swishing across the floor, and moves onto the terrace and into the avenue of old trees to merge into the dark shadows. People who have seen her have remarked on how unhappy she looks. She has also been seen near the ruins of a Romanesque arch, again in white, her dark hair flowing over a black shawl, and again somewhat disconsolate. When children are around, though, her mood lifts noticeably.

Bochym Manor – Helston

There is the ghost of another lady not too far away. On a side road off the A3083 to Lizard, is the ancient manor house of Bochym, so old it was mentioned in the Domesday roll in 1086. By the days of the Tudors, the Bochym family had become Lords of the Manor, but they then became supporters of a number of losing causes. John Bochym took part in the 'Prayer Book' Rebellion by the Cornish in 1549, which cost him his head, and during the Civil War their house became a place of refuge for Royalists.

Odd as it may seem, though, the ghost inhabiting this history-soaked place is neither a headless Bochym nor some swash-buckling Cavalier, but a 'Pink Lady'. She can be seen frequently in the suite in which she once lived – denting pillows, moving cutlery, rattling and shaking doors. Whether pink was her favourite colour, or whether she was wearing this particular dress when she died, we cannot say. No one has been able to identify her, but one story says she took her own life after her lover had been killed in a duel with her father. Whether this is so we cannot confirm, but a terrifying ghostly duel does take place nearby.

In the library at the Royal Cornwall Museum in Truro is an account of a supernatural occurrence written by Sub-Lieutenant Alfred Jelf of the Royal Navy. During World War I, he was stationed at the Royal Navy Mullion Air Station at Bonython, near Cury Cross Lanes, where he was involved in anti-submarine patrols and convoy support duties. On 15 October 1917, Jelf was given a 24-hour leave and as he walked towards Mullion to visit friends he stopped to admire a view of Bochym valley. There he was startled to see two figures in a field fighting a duel with long swords or rapiers.

They were wearing unmistakably Stuart clothes of short dark-green coats with light-coloured ruffs and caps with feathers, one with knee breeches. The contest was short, lasting only between three-quarters and one-and-a half minutes. As Jelf watched, one of the contestants was run through and fell to the ground, the other bent over him for a moment, rose, and beckoned six men from behind a hedge who put him in a coffin, before they all disappeared – except the victor who pointed his sword towards Jelf. Terrified, Jelf did not wait. Faster than ever before, he flew to his friend's house, where he arrived covered in mud and in a state of panic.

Had the Sub-Lieutenant had some form of hallucination brought on by exhaustion through flying too many stressful hours? He himself remained convinced that what he had seen was supernatural.

Don't be too sceptical. The duel has since been seen by many other people. Are the combatants the 'Pink Lady's' lover and her father? Or are the two events unconnected?

Antony House – Torpoint

Y ou wouldn't immediately pick out this corner of Cornwall as a maelstrom of spirits, but it does have an unusual ghost.

In October, 1880, Lady Helen Waldegrave came to visit the Carew Pole family at Antony House, bringing with her a Scottish maid, Helen Alexander. Young, shy and reserved, Helen didn't make friends with the other servants at the house though she did mention to one or two of them that she had a sister to whom she was writing while in Cornwall. Unfortunately, shortly after arriving, Helen became ill. Her health quickly deteriorated and the local doctor diagnosed typhoid fever. Until a trained nurse arrived, one of the permanent housemaids, Frances Reddel, was put in charge of looking after her.

Frances was different altogether, extravert, experienced and unflappable, and was not in the least perturbed as her patient's condition worsened and she was detailed to serve as night nurse as well. All was quiet in the bedroom, Helen slept fitfully and Frances was carrying out her normal routines. In the early hours of the morning, as she was preparing a dose of medicine which had to be administered at specific times, she was surprised when a stout, elderly lady came into the room without even knocking.

Even more puzzling was that the woman was wearing a long red nightgown over a red flannel petticoat and she was carrying an ornate brass candlestick. Frances even noticed a hole in the woman's petticoat, which she knew from her experience had been caused by stays rubbing inside. Frances was not the sort of girl to be alarmed by the woman's unexpected appearance and just assumed Helen's mother must have been sent for, without her being told – not an unusual occurrence in this particular house.

Frances watched as the visitor walked across the room without speaking, her eyes fixed straight ahead, sat on the bed and looked earnestly at her very sick daughter. She was though conscious that time was slipping by, so returned to preparing the medicine. But when she looked up towards Helen there was no trace of the woman who had been here only moments earlier! No one could have re-crossed that room and left without her knowing. It was just not possible.

Yet of the woman she had seen so plainly, there was no sign. However, Helen's condition was deteriorating so rapidly that Frances had to concentrate on her duties. All other thoughts went out of her mind. The doctor was called but could do nothing to help. By dawn, Helen Alexander was dead.

Two days later, Helen's family arrived from Scotland. Frances had the shock of her life. In every describable way, Helen's mother resembled exactly the figure she had seen visiting her dying patient at four o'clock in the morning the night Helen died. She told the other maids, but they were naturally sceptical.

Not until a few days later, as the grieving parents were preparing to leave, did anyone think of asking about the incident and only then of Helen's sister, Morag. What she revealed startled all the maids. Her mother did indeed have a nightgown exactly as Frances had described and a red flannel petticoat which she usually wore, and what's more it did have a hole where the stays had worn through!

Further still, her mother also had an unusually designed candlestick, even down to the small dent Frances had noticed and described! There was something else. When writing home to Morag, Helen had not mentioned her illness. No one had contacted them about it. Yet during the night when Helen died her mother had suddenly said to her husband that she was worried because their daughter was very ill.

It is difficult to explain such an incident. What had Frances seen? Was it something projected from the mind of the dying Helen, and how had she communicated with her mother?

And lastly a haunted field at...

Harlyn House - Trevose

Every year, thousands of people visit Mother Ivey's Bay, and probably pass the neglected wrought iron gates to Harlyn House. They then drive alongside an unremarkable field. It's an irregular shape, full of lumps and bumps, and grows only scrawny grass on which just a few sheep or cattle can graze – though it always has a good crop of nettles, thistles and weeds! But you would be advised to take notice. You see, this field is cursed.

It all started in 1632 when Thomas Peter of Treator, near Padstow, took over Harlyn House on his marriage to Elizabeth, only daughter and heiress of Henry Michell, whose family had owned it for a century and a half. The house you see today is nothing like it was then. Now it is a restored late-Georgian stone building with a date-stone for 1798. But its estate included the broad sweep of sandy downs above Harlyn Bay, and this included our fallow field. During the Civil War, Thomas Peter had fought on the losing Royalist side and from the time he was released from prison on February 2, 1653, he and his family displayed considerable entrepreneurial acumen, quickly enlarging and improving their estate. They also made huge profits from pilchard fishing.

Pilchards were one of the mainstays of the Cornish economy and a major part of the staple diet of most Cornishmen. A series of poor cereal harvests made food expensive and people even more dependent on pilchards. They were relieved when in 1794 the shoals arrived as normal and provided a particularly bountiful catch. Henry Peter of Harlyn House, Thomas's descendent, decided to export a large proportion to Italy. Three boats set out, fully loaded with barrels of pilchards for Naples. Here they found a glut of fish: no-one wanted theirs. They tried Civitavecchia, then Genoa, but everywhere was the same. There was only one thing to do: return with the cargo to feed the hungry folk back home in Harlyn.

By the time of their arrival, the barrels had been at sea for two months, mostly in Mediterranean heat. When they were opened, the fish had 'turned', already decaying. Their contents couldn't possibly be eaten. Henry Peter ordered the whole rotting catch to be spread on the fallow field and ploughed in as manure, to improve the soil and increase the crop yield. Better that than nothing. A silent, hungry crowd watched – to windward, of course – as for two whole days the fish were scattered and the field ploughed. Feelings became inflamed and people demanded what was left. Henry Peter wouldn't agree. The possibility of food poisoning, and the agonising death it was in those days, was too great. It was Mother Ivey who warned him of the dire consequences of what he was doing.

Then aged over sixty, Mother Martha Ivey was a 'charmer', a highly regarded position in Cornish communities at that time, the repository of local knowledge, wisdom and natural herbal cures. People regularly visited her small, cliff-side cottage above Polventon Bay (now Mother Ivey's Bay) where she had lived with her husband ever since their marriage. Her brother-in-law had died recently and left her his estate, in trust for her own sons. She regarded herself as the equal of Henry Peter. She would make sure he listened. We don't know how heated their discussion became. We can be sure she didn't curse him, for the Witchcraft Acts were still on the statute book and she had no wish to be imprisoned or worse still burned at the stake. But she did warn him. It was other people who said she laid a curse that if this fallow field is ever ploughed or dug again; one of the family owning it will die, unexpectedly.

Only a few years later, the curse took effect. Thomas Peter, eldest son of the then owner, an experienced rider, was thrown from his horse against a rock, and died almost instantly. A generation later and Charles Peter, again an eldest son, drowned whilst trying to cross the River Camel on a stormy night. Other members of the Peter family died unexpectedly, too. People said they always occurred after attempts to cultivate the fallow field, efforts which were always abortive.

After William Hellyar bought Harlyn House in 1886, our field was left rough for grazing and so his family escaped the curse – until 1941. Then, soldiers stationed nearby dug air-raid trenches across it. A week later, German bombs fell on Buckingham Palace, killing Harold Hellyar, the eldest son of the family, who was working there as an electrician. After the war, one evening in October, 1948, Jack Hellyar, now the eldest son, was walking home across the field when he was suddenly enveloped by a dark, dense, amorphous cloud-like form, evil and vengeful, from which he had great difficulty breaking free before stumbling across the field, exhausted.

Jack's father had ordered a labourer to dig a pond on the cliff-top. Whilst doing this he had unearthed a slate coffin which contained a few bones, a beaker and two discoloured but intact and magnificent Bronze Age ornaments. (These can be seen at the Royal Cornwall Museum in Truro). Breaking open the grave, however inadvertently, apparently had the same consequences as disturbing the fallow field. Jack Hellyar's experience was not the last. Several years later, Harlyn House was bought by Lt Cdr P Millar. Workmen carrying out renovations for him uncovered a small, unknown doorway, and all were terrified by the frightening atmosphere which emanated from it and surrounded them. They never returned. The curse remains operative.